YouTube Marketing

How to Create a Successful Channel and
Make Money

Table Of Contents

Introduction to YouTube 1

Chapter 1: YouTube Video Optimization 3

Chapter 2: Tips on Creating Great Videos 7

Chapter 3: Strategies for Growing Your Audience 11

Chapter 4: Making Money with YouTube 17

Chapter 5: Increasing YouTube Engagement 21

Chapter 6: YouTube Mistakes to Avoid 25

Conclusion 30

Introduction to YouTube

Many thought that YouTube was a trend that wasn't going to last. But shockingly, it has grown to become one of the biggest websites on the internet. And there is evidence to support that it will continue to rise. At the moment, over 1 billion people use it.

If you are a business, ignore YouTube at your own peril. Apart from SEO, SMM, and blogging, video marketing is a trend that will be a big part of internet marketing for a foreseeable future. And current technology is making it easier for customers to consume videos than ever before.

YouTube gives your business access to more customers. And this can give you an advantage over other businesses that do not include it in their marketing campaigns.

But YouTube isn't just for businesses, individuals can use it as well. All you need is an idea on what topics you will cover and the courage to do it. And you do not even need a website to get started.

But the biggest question you may have is whether it is possible to make serious money with YouTube. And the answer is yes! However, it depends on how hard you are willing to work. If you are lazy, then YouTube is not for you. Additionally, it is not a get-rich-quick scheme.

As someone who has created several YouTube channels, I know how frustrating it can be when getting started. Much of the information on the internet is not suitable for beginners. Furthermore, it can be confusing.

In this book, I will give you some tips on how you can have a successful YouTube channel. I will also give you tips on how you can make money with it. I'm sure you will find the book helpful.

Enjoy the reading.

Chapter 1: YouTube Video Optimization

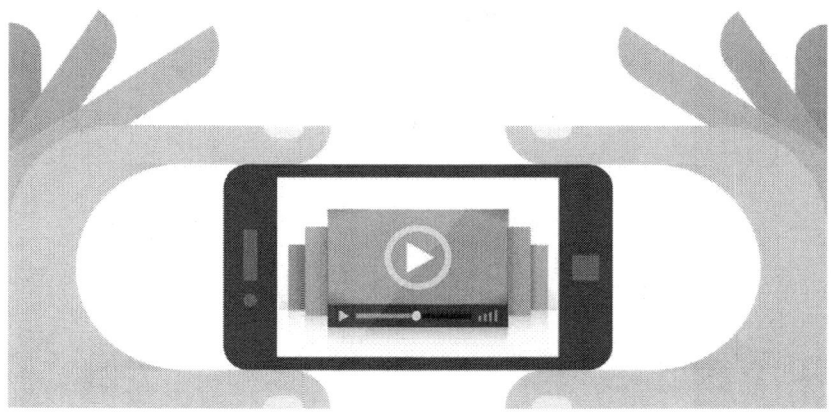

Over 300 hours of new videos are uploaded to YouTube every minute. For viewers, this is a blessing as they have a lot to watch. For video creators, unfortunately, that statistic should raise some hair. Standing out from such a cloud will take a lot of work.

But that doesn't mean it cannot be done. Actually, if others are doing it, why should you fail? One of the strategies you can use is optimization.

What Is Optimization

When looking for something on the internet, you think of some words you can use to search for that thing in a search engine. Those words are called keywords. For example, you would type "how to bake a cake" in Google. In this case, the keyword is "how to bake a cake."

When used in a video, the keyword informs the viewer about the content he will see. Also, since search engines can't watch a video, they rely on the keywords to understand it. This helps your video to rank in search results that contain the keyword.

With proper optimization, you can get a lot of viewers some of which may turn into subscribers. And this would lead to an increase in your income.

However, optimization isn't just about using any words. You must find the right ones in a process called keyword research. And this can be a lot of work depending on how competitive your niche is.

How Do You Find Keywords

You shouldn't wait for great keywords to land on your head like water on a rainy day. In the world of keywords, it doesn't rain every day.

You should look for words with high search volumes. At the same time, these words must be relevant to your video.

Here are some tips you can follow to find good keywords:

Ask people – you may start by asking others the words they would use if they were looking for something. Since they may not be familiar with the words you use in your industry, they will give you keywords average people would use. And you would be surprised with the results you can find with this method.

Come up with some words yourself – in addition to the words you would get from the people you ask, you must also think of some keywords yourself.

Spy at the competition – competitors make your work difficult, but they can also simplify it. If the competitors you focus on are big, chances are that they use some of the best keywords. Looking at their titles, descriptions, and the tags is a good way to get started.

Use a keyword tool – there are a lot of keyword tools you can use. These will give you a clear picture if the words you have chosen get enough searches to drive traffic to your channel. Some tools you can use include Wordtracker, SEObook.com, and AdWords Keyword Planner.

You should go for keywords with a minimum of 300 searches in a search engine like Google.

How to Use Keywords

Let's assume you have found some great keywords. Still, there is one important thing you should also master – knowing how to use them. No matter how great your keywords are, if you goof on this, you won't achieve anything. Here is how you can use keywords:

- Title – you must find a way to fit your keyword in this space. This is easier when the title has a couple of words.

- Description – don't be lazy and make a one sentence description like many newbies. You want your description to be of a good length. Ideally, it should be between 250-500 words. This will give you a chance to use the keywords without stuffing them. The keyword must be used 3 or 4 times.

- Tags – although not very important, you must not ignore them.

- Video name – you must rename your video so that it includes your main keyword.

Chapter 2: Tips on Creating Great Videos

Success on YouTube comes from doing a couple of things right. One such thing is giving your viewers what they want to see.

No matter how good your keywords are, or how powerful your camera is, you will not be a big hit if your videos suck. And it won't be long before you will start looking for another way to make money.

So you must do your best to avoid filling your channel with mediocre content.

Here are tips you can use:

Make a plan – I don't have to remind you that failing to prepare is preparing to fail. If you want to make a good video, you must write a plan of what you will say before you even get in front of the camera.

This will help keep your message focused. Also, you will have a chance to iron out imperfections on paper and not in the video. As if not enough, knowing what you will say will boost your confidence.

Make sure the video is relevant – even though people spend a lot of time on YouTube, it doesn't mean they are ready to consume garbage. So every video you post must have some benefit to them. Unfortunately, people are different; what's useful to you may not be useful to me.

To avoid that, determine your audience first. Are they women aged 20 who live in the U.K? Or are they middle-aged men interested in golf? Once you have this, you must determine their main purpose of watching your video. You can do this by reaching out to them and asking. If you don't have the resources, follow them on social media and see the things that trouble them.

For every video you post, you must ensure that it solves the problem you identified.

Work like an expert – YouTube is no longer a platform for teenage boys with a lot of free time. If you want professional looking videos, you must work like a professional. So instead of shooting the video yourself, you may hire a videographer. And instead of shooting in your bedroom, you can rent a studio. Although this may sound like a lot of money, you would be surprised how cheap it can be when compared to the benefits you get.

Use proper equipment – if you have to shoot the videos yourself, then you must use the right equipment. Unlike decades ago, it's now possible to find a decent camcorder in the $100 range. And if your phone has a good camera, you may also want to use that. But for the love of God, stay away from your computer's webcam.

Another thing you will want is a mic. USB microphones have also come down in price – so no excuses. And if you will be working indoors, you will need some lights.

Know how to edit – you must shoot your videos so that they won't require much post processing. However, editing is still something you should embrace. It will give your videos a professional feel by enhancing things or correcting some mistakes.

Unfortunately, learning to edit properly takes time. But you can accelerate your progress by reading a lot on this topic and practicing at every chance you get.

Have a good title – before anyone will decide to watch your video, he will look at your title first. So you should take your time when crafting this. But don't get clever here – your title should describe the video. Good titles are short, have keywords, and still communicate what the video is about without losing the viewer's interest.

Choose a good thumbnail – along with a good title, you must ensure that you have also chosen a good thumbnail for your video. Although you are free to go with the one YouTube chooses, you will get more views with a custom thumbnail. Even better, you can have a still image that captures the most attractive part of your video. If this was a recipe, you can have a picture of the food.

Your content should be unique – you do not need to go to mars to discover fresh ideas. Even if something has been done 100 times, there are still another 100 ways to do it differently. So decide how you can present the message in your video from a new angle.

Shoot with two cameras – in order to make your video less boring, you may want to invest in a second camera. By changing viewing angles, you will make your videos interesting.

Make a proper intro and ending – an intro is a good way to introduce viewers to your channel. Also, it puts them at ease and gives them a sense that you take your work seriously. An ending encourages them to subscribe to your channel, share, comment, or like the video.

Chapter 3: Strategies for Growing Your Audience

If you have a lot of subscribers on your channel, making money with YouTube won't be a far-fetched dream. Every video you will upload will have people waiting to watch it.

However, to grow your audience, you don't have to only rely on search engines for optimizing your videos as we discussed in chapter 1.

Here are other ways you can use:

Upload videos regularly – consistency is one of the strategies for getting a lot of subscribers. The funny thing is, it's so easy to understand this but difficult to practice it. However, you must still force yourself to create great content all the time. Also, you must have a schedule for when you upload videos to your channel. This will help your viewers know when to expect something new.

For fresh ideas, you can:

- see what your competitors are doing and find something to improve
- see the problems your audience complains about on social networks, forums, and Q&A sites
- talk to your audience directly, just one member is enough
- watch videos not related to your niche, you may get some inspiration or find an idea related to your niche
- think of the future and how it will affect your niche

Build links to your channel – if you have a blog with good traffic, you can make posts that are related to your videos. You would then embed the videos in the posts.

In addition, you can also embed the videos in a guest post on other sites. The more authoritative these websites are, the better. Furthermore, you can answer questions on websites like Quora, and provide a link to your video.

Ask for shares – even when viewers like your video, chances of sharing it are very low. But you can make them simply by asking. If the video entertained or informed them, they will likely respond positively to your request.

Having them share the video will carry more weight than if you do it. People trust recommendations from friends than strangers.

Let people subscribe from your website – assuming you have a website, you can let people subscribe to your YouTube channel from it. And this strategy is easy to implement as you just need to add a YouTube widget on your website.

However, this widget should be placed where it can easily be seen. Throwing it at the bottom is suicide because people don't usually get to the bottoms of web pages. Again, burying it amidst ads will be a waste of useful space.

Do cross promotion – it's normal to think of your competitors as enemies. Not only do they steal your subscribers, but they also contribute to making you go broke. However, you must remember that you are in business. A scratch on your competitor's back may get you one in return.

YouTube lets you have featured channels where you can include channels that may be useful to your subscribers. The owners of those channels may also add you as a featured channel, giving you access to some of their subscribers. This makes for a win-win situation.

Use annotations wisely – these are meant to correct mistakes in a video. Usually, these are minor mistakes that don't warrant reshooting the video. But you can use annotations as ads.

For starters, you can reinforce your call to action with these. For example, as the video is getting to the end, you can have an annotation that asks viewers to subscribe, share, comment or click a link.

Just don't get carried away in using them; a little goes a long way.

Ask for favors from your biggest fans – YouTube has a feature that lets you see your biggest fans. The keyword here is fans. They like your content and will be more than happy to help your channel reach new heights. So reach out to them and ask if they would love to promote your channel to their friends.

To make it easy for your fans, you can give them messages they should send to their friends.

Give incentives – this is a well-known strategy that can get you a lot of subscribers in no time. Who doesn't like free stuff? You can say by liking, sharing, or commenting on your video, someone will get a chance to win a gift.

However, the biggest disadvantage with this is that you will also attract other subscribers who are not interested in your content.

Create a channel trailer – a decision to watch a movie is usually influenced by a good trailer. Likewise, if you want to get a lot of subscribers, you should consider making a trailer. Every time a non-subscriber comes to your channel, he will be greeted with it. And if it's good, you can convert him into a subscriber.

Trailers showcase what you have to offer. And they make good tools for carrying your call to actions.

However, you must think of duration when creating your trailer. Although there is no limit, it's common knowledge that shorter is better. Specifically, don't let it exceed 90 seconds.

Don't ignore social media – social networking site aren't platforms to brag about how great your last weekend was. For YouTubers, you can use these sites as serious business tools. The best part is that a lot of people are now on social networking sites, giving you access to a wider audience.

Since you are just getting started, you may be overwhelmed with the number of social networks. But you do not need to have accounts in all of them.

First, determine your audience and know the social networking sites they use. You will likely end up with a long list of websites. From this, choose the best 2 or 3 sites to focus on. This will give you a chance to have time for growing your YouTube channel while still leveraging social media.

When you have a new video, you must share it on your social accounts. And YouTube makes this process easy.

Chapter 4: Making Money with YouTube

Making money with YouTube is no tea party. Knowing what to do is not enough. You need to apply the things you know. And this can be an uphill battle, especially for the faint-hearted.

Although there are a lot of ways you can use to make money with YouTube, some of those ways just don't work. They will waste your time and kill your morale when you see no adjustments in your account balance.

However, there are still other ways you can use. In this chapter, I will show you these ways. Just be ready to give them the effort they deserve.

Sponsored Video

This is one of the most lucrative ways of making money on YouTube. Just that YouTube has recently tightened the rules on it.

With this, you need to find yourself a sponsor. Your sponsor would then pay you to feature him or his products in your videos.

If you have a lot of subscribers, you can find a wealthy sponsor capable of paying you a lot of money. Also, great negotiation skills can help land you a nice contract.

But YouTube wants a piece of the cake. So to make sponsored videos without limitations, your sponsor must buy ads from Google. Those sponsors who don't will find this strategy less rewarding.

Whatever the case, you must only sponsor brands you trust. Promoting mediocre products to your subscribers because you want money will hurt your reputation and the success of your channel.

Drive Traffic to Your Website

This does not directly make you any money on YouTube. Instead, you work so hard providing free stuff on YouTube so you can drive people to your website. This is where your money making opportunities lie. Assuming your website is monetized, the traffic from YouTube can make you some money.

Current statistics show that over 1 billion people use YouTube. This makes it one of the greatest sources of traffic.

Do Affiliate Marketing

Another great way to make money is to focus on affiliate marketing. This means you will promote products of companies and get a commission on each sale made. The easy part is that you don't have to go through the labor of making any products yourself.

Although the commissions are usually low, the money can add up if you have a lot of videos and viewers.

When you register as an affiliate marketer, you are given a unique link. This enables the website you are working for to track your earnings.

Just like with sponsored videos, you must choose products you believe in. And this is easy since you have a whole range of products to choose from.

You can make reviews about the product, videos showing how to use it, or any kind of video you know your subscribers will like. You would then insert your affiliate link in the video.

Become a YouTube Partner

This is probably the easiest way to get started making money on YouTube. The only drawback is that it does not make a lot of money for most people. As a YouTube partner, you agree to have ads in your videos. These are placed by YouTube and you split the money made.

In order to be successful with this strategy, you need to have a lot of videos on your channel. At the same time, you also need a lot of viewers.

Promote Your Own Products

If you have a book, software, or anything you would like to sell, you are free to use YouTube for promoting it. This is similar to affiliate marketing. The only difference is all the money belongs to you instead of getting a small piece of the cake.

Chapter 5: Increasing YouTube Engagement

Engagement is one thing you shouldn't ignore on YouTube. Remember, this website isn't just a platform for hosting your videos; it is a community. The more you engage with others, the more fun it becomes.

But engagement isn't only important as a way of finding new friends living in another continent. It is also used by YouTube to determine your rank. Lots of likes, comments, and shares show that you have a great video. And this makes YouTube include it in search results.

So you must approach this topic seriously. Unfortunately, since your channel is just new, the handful of subscribers you have may be reluctant in engagement. This is when you must wear the hat of a true marketer. You must use tactics that increase the possibility of healthy engagement.

Here are some tips you can use:

Have a personality – no one will want to establish engagement if it feels like there is a robot behind your channel. People want to interact with other people. So in your videos, try to show your human side. I know making money is serious business, but that doesn't have to take all the fun away.

For a start, you can try to be less formal. You can laugh, make jokes, show your bloopers, and anything you believe your audience will connect with. You don't have to be perfect; that is something for computers.

A common mistake is to try to be someone else. Unfortunately, your viewers will see through this and it may make you look awkward. You have to remember that there is no one like you. And this is the reason your viewers tuned in. They want to see you and your ideas.

Ask for engagement – as said in chapter 3, people need a little push to do things. Usually, no matter how great your video is, your viewers will not think of commenting on their own.

So what do you have to do? Simply ask! And there is no reason to feel like you are being desperate by doing this. Everybody does it.

However, you don't just need to ask anyhow. This is your call to action, so you have to properly plan it if you want the best results.

Making a great call to action is not easy. You must tell the viewers the benefit they will get for doing what you are asking from them. For example, telling them how much you will appreciate if they will comment on your video is a good way to start. But you have to think outside the box for even better results.

Respond to Comments - if someone comments on your video, they like your content (assuming it's a positive comment). And the last thing you want is to not respond to such good comments. You will kill engagement faster than you think.

But if you respond, you will please your viewers. The next time you will have a new video, they will be more than happy to comment again. This will lead to a stronger relationship, which is crucial for your success. Also, by seeing the interaction on your channel, new subscribers will be willing to join in the fun.

But you shouldn't just respond to positive comments, the negatives ones also matter. Just try to be polite and never take anything seriously.

Know the Needs of Your Audience - this may seem like an off-topic addition only included to make the chapter longer. But it's not. In fact, it is among the most important strategies for increasing engagement.

No one will be willing to share, like, or comment on your video if it wasn't of any benefit to him. So when making your videos, you have to think of your viewers. Determine what they want to watch.

Although you can just guess this, it's better to have a chat with a member of your audience. If that's not an option, follow them on social networks to know their problems.

And when you finish making your videos, you have to think if those videos achieve what you customers wished for.

Ask questions – your viewers may have knowledge on something you do not know. Instead of researching that thing yourself, you would just ask them to share what they know about the subject. With the right questions, you can give birth to healthy conversations.

Cover current events – this strategy is easy to implement and can give you great results. On your part, you have to be in touch with everything going on in your industry. You can do this by reading news, following the industry leaders, attending special events, etc.

Chapter 6: YouTube Mistakes to Avoid

If you will do something wrong a couple of times, a moment will come when you will learn how to do it right. The only drawback is that this may derail you. Additionally, if you are like others, you may give up before achieving your goal.

Since you are on YouTube to make money, you don't want mistakes to hold you back. Others have already been there so you can learn from their mistakes. This will help reduce the time it will take before you start making money on YouTube.

Having Unrealistic Expectations

New YouTubers have hyped up expectations of what success is like on YouTube. They believe that, if they have a good video, it will get lots of views and make a lot of money.

If you have that mindset too, you must slow down a little. Your work does not end when you finally upload your video. Actually, uploading your video marks the beginning of a new phase that needs even more work. Specifically, you will need to promote your video. And even then, don't think you will start making money right away. It takes time.

Focusing Too Much on Short Videos

Knowing what to include in your videos to make them valuable comes with experience. As a result, you may find that most of your videos will be shorter since you are just getting started. But such videos don't usually cut it.

To begin with, they do not give the viewer enough information to help him. For example, you cannot make a decent review of your brand new phone that lasts for 1 minute. Secondly, search engines prefer longer videos in their search results. Searching "how to draw a cartoon character" in Google brought results that are longer than 3 minutes.

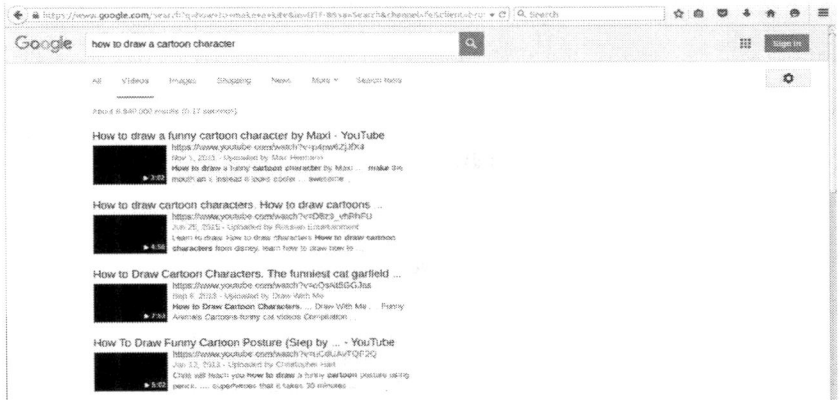

However, this doesn't mean you should include fluff just to make the video longer. Viewers won't be patient to stick till the end. And this will also hurt since YouTube uses the percentage of the video watched as an indicator of quality.

A research by Buffer Social has indicated that the ideal video length is 2 min 54 seconds. But that should not limit your creativity. You can make a video that is longer than 3 minutes as long as you have reasons to justify it. I have seen videos that are 1 hour long and still manage to get lots of views.

Neglecting Audio Quality

Most people can stand a bad video. But it's only a handful of them who will put up with bad audio. And this may seem confusing since we think of the image as being more important than the audio. But the truth is that audio also matters.

Like I said earlier, you must get a stand alone mic. This will sound better than your camcorder's built-in microphone.

Additionally, you must record in a room that is not noisy. Closing the windows and doors should help eliminate most of the sounds outside. Also, you may want to use a pop filter to reduce popping sounds.

If you find it impossible to record audio as you shoot the video, then start with the video, and do the audio latter.

Being Everything

No one will want to subscribe to your channel if it has no main theme. It could be that you have videos on sports, fashion, music, tech products, make money-online tutorials, etc.

Instead, you must have a channel for every niche you want to cover. This will make it easier to reach your target audience.

Selling Too Much

Although ads can be fun to watch, the fact still remains that they suck. And the last thing viewers want is to tune into a channel only to be bombarded with lots of advertisements.

You are free to sell as much as you want, but try to keep a balance between selling and giving your customers what they want. If you don't sell too much, you will find it easy to win the loyalty of your customers. And this will help you make more money.

Editing Too Much

Excessive editing screams "amateur work." No amount of post processing will make your video great if it is bad in the first place. So you must focus on getting a good video when shooting. This will eliminate the need for too much editing.

There is a breed of YouTubers that just can't keep their hands from the mouse. They add so many effects to the video that instead of watching it, you are left wondering if all this was necessary.

Here is a rule you should always remember - only edit if you know what you are doing will enhance your video.

Conclusion

I would like to thank you for reading the book. I'm sure you now know how you can create a successful channel and make money with it. If you do everything right, the dream of making money with YouTube will become a reality.

However, the lessons from this book are of no use if you won't turn them into actions.

Success on YouTube does not come easy. You will need to work very hard. That is, you must be on the hunt for new ideas and do your best to produce great videos every time. Furthermore, you must not forget to promote your channel. Although you can make money with YouTube, it won't happen overnight. So be patient and don't lose hope.

You must also keep on learning. You may do this by being friends with fellow YouTubers; they may know something you don't. Additionally, the internet provides most of the things you may need to know about YouTube, so make full use of it.

You don't have to wait till you are perfect to become a YouTuber. You will learn the other things you don't know along the way. So get started today. I wish you luck in your quest to making money with YouTube.

Made in the USA
Lexington, KY
18 November 2016